THE WALL ST. INSIDERS' JOKE BOOK

THE WALL ST. INSIDERS' JOKE BOOK

Buffy Bluechip

CROWN PUBLISHERS, INC., NEW YORK

Published by Crown Publishers, Inc.,
225 Park Avenue South, New York, New York 10003
and represented in Canada by the Canadian MANDA Group

CROWN is a trademark of Crown Publishers, Inc.

Manufactured in the United States of America

Library of Congress Cataloging-in-Publication Data

Bluechip, Buffy.
The Wall St. insiders' joke book / Buffy Bluechip.
p. cm.
1. Stocks—Anecdotes, facetiae, satire, etc. 2. Wall Street—Anecdotes, facetiae, satire, etc. 3. Investments—Anecdotes, facetiae, satire, etc. 4. Finance—Anecdotes, facetiae, satire, etc. I. Title. II. Title: Wall St. insiders' joke book.
HG4528.B58 1988
332.6'0207—dc19 87-30508 CIP
ISBN 0-517-56877-2 (pbk.)

10 9 8 7 6 5 4 3 2 1

First Edition

Contents

INTRODUCTION

I heard the first Gary Hart jokes in London almost immediately after the headlines proclaimed his association with Donna Rice last May. I'd been interviewing some analysts at the investment firm Salomon Brothers, and one of the traders strolled in with the question:

What do Gary Hart and Prime Minister Nakasone have in common?
Both eat rice

Where did that joke start? Was it born in Salomon Brothers' London office? No, the trader told me he heard it from New York, where it was still early morning and where Wall Street's cadre of traders and brokers had just arrived at work and begun reading the headlines. So I called a trader in Sali's New York office, who said he had heard the joke from a mutual friend of ours at Prebon. I called him and he said he thought the joke started at Kidder, Peabody, where one individual in particular is known for his creative punch lines. (No name, he *really* does want to be an investment banker, not the next star of "Saturday Night Live.") I called our friend at Kidder and he denied authorship.

By this time, the joke was being told around the world, thanks to the vast telephone network that links

Wall Street to every other trading floor on the globe, and allows traders to chat away to foreign countries at all hours of the day and night. With more and more people telling the joke, the variations started. For one, the joke united two top news stories of that week: Gary Hart's blunder and the Japanese domination of the financial markets. The Japanese link and a play on Donna Rice's last name offered new possibilities. The next jokes on the humor mill evolved as:

What did Prime Minister Nakasone say to Gary Hart?
Congraturations on your next erection

What's Gary Hart's new diet?
The Rice Diet

Then Hart's gaffe was linked to history:

What was his biggest mistake?
That he didn't let Teddy Kennedy drive Donna home

That kind of gallows humor put Hart into the high ranks of fallen politicos with the joke:

Did you hear about the new law firm Richard Nixon, Gary Hart, and Teddy Kennedy formed?
Trick 'em, Dick 'em, and Dunk 'em

"We'd like to take credit for that one, we really would," said my source at Kidder. "But just don't use any of our names." I tried to convince him otherwise, but got even more reasons for protecting their identities. "It could probably ruin our careers," he said, sounding panicked. "Who would admit to making up any of these kinds of jokes?"

As a financial journalist, I had encountered a source's reluctance to go on the record before, but his remark made quite an impression on me, so much so that I even thought about *my* career (hence, my pen name, Buffy Bluechip). But it wasn't enough to make me give up my pursuit of finding out where these off-the-news jokes actually originate. With each new Hart joke, I faced up to the challenge of Wall Street's network of telephone contacts that creates its daily business dealings: a broker who knows a trader who knows a dealer knows a broker who knows a dealer who told the joke first. It became a little like tracing a serial murder suspect.

After a couple of days of calling around, I concluded that a good joke travels faster than the speed of sound as more and more people tell it. Meanwhile my fingertips were getting raw from punching numbers on my Touch-tone telephone. I smartened up, decided simply to get the jokes from anyone who could remember them, and let it go at that.

As a result, this book took months of dogged devotion to the world of high finance. A lot of the jokes probably were invented by traders on Wall Street, and all of the jokes came from people who work there, usually from the crowd that congregates every Friday night at South Street Seaport, the yuppie hangout downtown. After a few beers, they had more than enough jokes to relate, even if they couldn't remember where they had heard them first. Jokes are such a great way to warm a client to a sale that some brokers even pulled out ragged index cards from their wallets with the latest punch lines scribbled down for quick reference.

The jokes tend to fall into two categories: the day-to-day variety—ethnic jokes, jokes about sex, marriage, or the office—which are so commonly told that I didn't attribute the jokes to any source in particular, and the calamity jokes. Calamity humor, such as the Gary Hart jokes, is more creative and comes in waves, since it is right off the news. All at once, about twenty jokes on the Ethiopian famine can hit the market and go through twists and turns as they are told and retold at least two hundred times by brokers from Wall Street to London to Long Island to New Jersey to Los Angeles to Tokyo. Then all that hilarity fades away until the next big event.

A lot of the humor is sort of tasteless but sort of fun, as well. There's more than one reason for Wall Street's generic brand of humor. One is that the workplace is still dominated by men, and the humor is often aggressive, release oriented, a civilized alternative to violence. Or at least that's what the shrinks say. I see it as a way to cope with the everyday pressure of dealing in the topsy-turvy stock and bond markets. After all, these are the kinds of people who can lose a million in one second. One misjudgment, one ticker later, and their balance sheets can go into the doghouse along with their reputations.

Uncertainty, then, is the nature of the game. Wall Street is a gamblers' den with platoons of traders and brokers trying to figure out what the other guy is going to do next. And the best way to deal with that kind of tension is a kind of thumbs-up attitude. It's got to be fun or you wouldn't be doing your job. If it were too much, you'd hang yourself. In fact, Wall Street was known for its hilarity even back in Ben Franklin's time, when Wall Street was just an open-air market. Some of the humor took a more poetic form than today's standard joke: "He that sells what isn't his'n either pays or goes to prison" is a famous couplet invented on Wall Street about selling short. Jocularity also took the form of sing-alongs. "The men of the Exchange were known for their daily merriment," recounts one stockbroker in his diary of Wall Street wheelings and dealings in the nineteenth century.

So the contemporary equivalent of this ballroom chorus is the joke, which, despite the geographic source, has a universal appeal. That's because the context of the humor—the marketplace—is sort of like life itself. After all, Wall Street is a thoroughfare that starts in the graveyard of Trinity Church and ends in the East River. Like life, it's a place where its members never know what's coming down the pike. Humor is an essential weapon not only to survive the uncertainty of that kind of business environment, but also to cope with the world outside of work, as well. One way around the darker side of life can be to approach it playfully. We can all acknowledge the tragedy of the *Challenger* disaster, and the jokes are one way of coping with this horrible reminder of life's unfairness. And they really do tickle the funny bone.

That's because humor, like truth, is a great equalizer. It can successfully defy convention, tackle taboos, and transform anxieties into absurdities, whether it be over nuclear disasters like Chernobyl or tragedies like Leon Klinghoffer's death. Wall Street also recognizes what isn't funny. Oliver North and the Iran-contra hearings weren't absurd enough to trigger any jokes, and Ronald Reagan has become a King Lear; the humor went out of the White House the minute Reagan started forgetting his own punch lines.

Humor is also a way for Wall Streeters to boost their own morale in these scandal-drenched times. E.F. Hutton, for one, spent fifty thousand dollars on producing a coloring book for its employees as a way to fight off its tarnished reputation over a huge trading loss and lawsuits. Firms such as Drexel Burnham Lambert, whose image has been blackened by the insider-trading scandal that rocked Wall Street last year, have yet to resort to such tactics, but some of the best jokes about Drexel originated right from its own trading floor.

And even though these people make a ton of money, they work for it. The real nature of their work is as routine as it is time pressured. Jokes are a way to relieve the boredom of eight to five and, in some cases, eight to eleven. That's why, on a down day, commonly known as a bear market, humor is a way to cope with a hit to the profit-and-loss statement. Some bears are also incredibly slow days, and that's when some of the most creative jokes are born. On a fast day or rising market, known as a bull, the humor is swift and obvious; no one wants to waste time on puns or real words if a bid-ask spread needs to be quoted that could put some money in the firm's bonus pool.

Ironically enough, in my research I found that, aside from Wall Street, the strongest flow of jokes right now comes out of Eastern Europe, where humor is a form of political therapy to cope with tyranny. Seen from that perspective, Wall Street's brand of humor—as tasteless, sexist, and racist as it sometimes is—seems a gleeful diversion. And that's the key to appreciating it.

Special thanks go to: Mark G., Tom W., Ellen I., Mark W., Andy C., David M., Ray, David F., James S., Peter M., Tom F., T.J., Jody W., Harlen S., Courtney M., Kevin G., Nancy C., John M., the bartenders of Fluties at South Street Seaport, Delmonico's, and Tom M., Dan, and Jim, the California consultants.

The Market Makers: Wall Street on the Headlines

Most Wall Streeters are news junkies, since the markets usually generate the first wide response to any crisis. Violence breaks out in the Middle East and oil prices can skyrocket. So it's important that Wall Streeters keep abreast of breaking news. And that's pretty easy. Reuters screens span the walls of many trading rooms, while each broker and trader also has access to the news wires via computer screens on the trading desks. It is no wonder, then, that Wall Street is also a great source of jokes about news events?

"When something comes across the wire that looks like it could generate some jokes, we take bets about how many minutes—or even seconds—will pass before we hear the first," said one broker. Either the telephone rings with a tidal wave of puns, or in-house comedians come up with their own versions. Sometimes the news wires also run the jokes, if they aren't too offensive. Of course, they usually are.

The best punch lines stick in everyone's memories, although the news events themselves may be harder to recall, so I've dug up some headlines to make the jokes as freshly funny as when they first broke through.

MORE THAN SEVEN MILLION
FACE STARVATION IN ETHIOPIA
***New York Times,* August 21, 1986**

What's the world's fastest animal?
An Ethiopian chicken
BROKER, MKI MONEY MARKETS

Who's the patron saint of Ethiopia?
Karen Carpenter
IBID.

What do you call fifty Ethiopians carrying a canoe?
A comb
IBID.

What do you call an Ethiopian with a swollen big toe?
A three wood
IBID.

What do you call an Ethiopian with buck teeth?

A rake

IBID.

What are venetian blinds used for in Ethiopia?

Bunk beds

IBID.

What do you call an Ethiopian walking a dog?

Full

IBID.

What do you call an Ethiopian walking two dogs?

A caterer

IBID.

What do you call an Ethiopian walking three dogs?

A vegetarian

IBID.

What's the most useless thing in Ethiopia?

An after-dinner mint

TRADER, FIRST BOSTON

What do you call an Ethiopian with a sesame seed on his head?

A quarter-pounder

BANKER, BANK OF NEW YORK

How can you tell a wealthy Ethiopian?

He's wearing the solid-gold Rolex around his waist.

BANKER, CHEMICAL BANK

What do you call an Ethiopian with a hat on?

A Nail

IBID.

HERPES: HALF OF ALL ADULTS MAY HAVE IT

***New York Times,* June 15, 1986**

What's the difference between herpes and true love?

Herpes lasts forever.

GOVERNMENT BOND TRADER,
MORGAN STANLEY

AIDS Epidemic Continues Unabated: Some Medical Experts Fear That Disease May Now Pose Threat to Heterosexuals

***New York Times,* January 22, 1985**

What's the AIDS diet?

The only food that slips under a locked door: pancakes and flounder

INVESTMENT BANKER,
PRUDENTIAL-BACHE

Suspect in L.A. Freeway Shootings Found with Help of Cyclist

***New York Times,* August 4, 1987**

Have you heard about the new bumper sticker on the Los Angeles expressway?

"I break for reloading."

BROKER, SAITAMA BANK

French Court Finds Barbie Guilty

***New York Times,* July 4, 1987**

Did you hear Klaus Barbie had a heart attack?

He got his gas bill from 1943.

BROKER, SHEARSON LEHMAN

JOHN DELOREAN IS CHARGED WITH POSSESSION OF MORE THAN 59 LBS. OF COCAINE: FBI INVESTIGATORS SAY HE WAS FINANCIER OF SCHEME TO SELL 220 LBS. OF COCAINE IN EFFORT TO SHORE UP HIS FINANCIALLY TROUBLED AUTO COMPANY IN NORTHERN IRELAND

***New York Times,* October 20, 1982**

What kind of tires does a DeLorean have?
Snow tires

GOVERNMENT BOND TRADER,
MORGAN STANLEY

Did your hear about the DeLorean?
It's the only car that goes "toot, toot."

IBID.

What do they call a DeLorean?
A snowmobile

IBID.

Did you hear about how a DeLorean drives?
The white line disappears on the road.

IBID.

TOLL 3,000 AND RISING IN BANGLADESH CYCLONE; ISLANDS RAVAGED BY STORM AND TIDAL WAVE

***Los Angeles Times*, May 28, 1985**

Hear about the new favorite music in Bangladesh?

New Wave

TRADER, MORGAN STANLEY

HARVEY MILK, SAN FRANCISCO'S FIRST ACKNOWLEDGED HOMOSEXUAL OFFICIAL, IS SHOT TO DEATH IN CITY HALL

***New York Times*, November 28, 1978**

Did you hear about the Harvey Milk school?

◇ *There was no principal, just a headmaster.*

◇ *They didn't have a football team, just tight ends.*

◇ *The baseball team was no good because they were all switch-hitters.*

◇ *There were no written exams, just oral.*

◇ *The school had no front door; the entrance was in the rear.*

◇ *The favorite game was "Swallow the leader."*

INVESTMENT BANKER, GOLDMAN SACHS

U.S. BELIEVES BODY WASHED UP ON SYRIAN COAST IS ALMOST CERTAINLY THAT OF LEON KLINGHOFFER, HOSTAGE REPORTEDLY SHOT BY HIJACKERS OF SHIP *ACHILLE LAURO*

***New York Times,* October 16, 1985**

Hear about the new Klinghoffer drink?
Two shots and a splash

TRADER, KIDDER, PEABODY

What did the sharks say when Leon splashed by?
It's a meal on wheels.

IBID.

Why didn't Leon shower that day?
He knew he'd wash up on shore.

FOREIGN EXCHANGE DESK,
PREBON MONEY BROKERS

What's PLO stand for?
Push Leon Over.

IBID.

Why was the wheelchair found by the Libyans?

If it had been found by the Jews, it would have been sold.

IBID.

What's worse than being captured by the PLO?

Being rescued by the Egyptians

IBID.

SPACE SHUTTLE *CHALLENGER* SHORTLY AFTER 11:39 A.M. LAUNCH FROM CAPE CANAVERAL, EXPLODES IN BALL OF FIRE AND ALL SEVEN ASTRONAUTS ON BOARD ARE KILLED

***New York Times*, January 29, 1986**

What's NASA stand for?

◇ *Need Another Seven Astronauts*

◇ *Now Accepting Seven Applications*

ARBITRAGEUR, SHEARSON LEHMAN

What's the #1 drink of the *Challenger*?

◇ *Ocean Spray*

◇ *Teacher's, Seven-Up, and a splash*

What's the last thing the astronauts of the *Challenger* said?

"I meant a Bud Lite!"

What do they call the bottom of the ocean floor near Cape Canaveral?

Astro-Turf

What were Christa McAuliffe's last words to her family?

"You feed the dog, I'll feed the fish."

What color were Christa McAuliffe's eyes?

Blue: One blew that way and the other blew this way.

What do the *Challenger* and the New England Patriots have in common?

Both looked good for the first fifty seconds.

What's worse than finding glass in your baby food?

Astronaut in your tuna fish

Where is Christa McAuliffe vacationing this summer?

All over Florida

Why was there only one black man on the *Challenger*?

Because they didn't know it would blow up

What was the last thing to go through the captain of the *Challenger*'s mind?

Christa McAuliffe's foot

What were Christa McAuliffe's last words?

"What's this button for?"

Why did the *Challenger* blow up?

That's what happens when you let a woman drive.

Where's the best place to watch the next shuttle launch?

A glass-bottomed boat

PRECEDING *CHALLENGER* JOKES
THANKS TO THE STAFF OF FLUTIES

What do walruses, Tylenol, and the *Challenger* have in common?

All are looking for a tight seal.

FOREX DESK, PREBON

Why was Christa McAuliffe such a good teacher?

She only blew up in front of her class once.

TRADER, MORGAN STANLEY

U.S. CONDUCTS SERIES OF AIR STRIKES IN LIBYA

***New York Times,* April 15, 1986**

What's the five-day forecast in Tripoli?

Three days

TRADER, SALOMON BROTHERS

JOHN LENNON, ONE OF THE BEATLES, IS SHOT AND KILLED WHILE ENTERING APARTMENT BUILDING WHERE HE LIVED

***New York Times,* December 9, 1980**

What would it take to get the Beatles back together?

Three more bullets

TRADER, FIRST BOSTON

What's yellow and sleeps alone?

Yoko Ono

IBID.

PAROLED RAPIST IS WELCOME NOWHERE

***New York Times,* May 28, 1987**

Did you hear Larry Singleton was picked up again?

For selling arms to the contras

FROM VARIOUS SOURCES

Captives, Body Parts Found in Philadelphia; Heidnik Arrested in Kidnapping and Rape

***New York Times,* March 27, 1987**

Why did accused murderer Gary Heidnik cut up but not cook the prostitutes' brains?

Because the United Negro College Fund says a mind is a terrible thing to baste

TRADER, MORGAN STANLEY

What's the new dog food invented in Philadelphia?

GALPO

IBID.

What's the new favorite dessert in Philadelphia?

Lady Fingers

IBID.

What's the new fashion line in Philadelphia?

Dismembers Only

IBID.

POLICE BOMB MOVE HEADQUARTERS IN PHILADELPHIA

***New York Times,* May 16, 1985**

How many Operation MOVE people can you fit into a VW?

Two in the front, two in the back, and eight in the ashtray

TRADER, MORGAN STANLEY

BABY FAE, INFANT WHO RECEIVED HEART OF BABOON 20 DAYS AGO TO REPLACE HER OWN DEFECTIVE HEART, DIES

***New York Times,* November 16, 1984**

What's faster than an Ethiopian chicken?

A baboon running past a heart clinic

BANKER, GOLDMAN SACHS

TOXIC GAS LEAK FROM UNION CARBIDE PLANT IN BHOPAL, INDIA, KILLS 400

***New York Times,* December 4, 1984**

What's Union Carbide's new theme song?

"One Little, Two Little, Three Little Indians"

TRADER, MORGAN STANLEY

Soviet Union Reports Accident at Chernobyl Nuclear Power Plant Which Spreads Radioactive Material

***New York Times,* April 29, 1986**

How many Russians does it take to screw in a lightbulb?

None. They all glow in the dark.

BROKER, SMITH BARNEY

What's the favorite drink in Chernobyl?

Black Russian

IBID.

What cackles and glows in the dark?

Chicken Kiev

IBID.

What's the new Russian currency?

The rubble

IBID.

Did you hear about the baby boom in Sweden?

Babies born with blue hair and blond eyes

IBID.

What do you use to clean up after a nuclear fallout?

Mop 'n' Glow

IBID.

PRESIDENT SADAT IS SHOT AND KILLED BY GROUP OF MEN IN MILITARY UNIFORMS AS HE WATCHES MILITARY PARADE IN CAIRO

***New York Times,* October 7, 1981**

What was the theme song at Sadat's funeral?

"I Love a Parade"

TRADER, MORGAN STANLEY

AIR FLORIDA JETLINER CRASHES INTO 14TH ST. BRIDGE AND BREAKS AS IT PLUNGES INTO THE POTOMAC

***New York Times,* January 14, 1982**

Before the crash, the pilot said to the crew: "I have good news and I have bad news. The good news is free drinks for everyone. The bad news is we have to stop at the bridge for ice."

ANALYST, WORLD BANK

What's Air Florida's new slogan?

Take the plane to the bridge.

FROM VARIOUS SOURCES

BUILDING COLLAPSE IN CONNECTICUT: A COMMUNITY GRIEVES

***New York Times,* April 26, 1987**

Did you hear that the funniest construction workers are in Bridgeport, Connecticut?

They bring the house down.

BROKER, OPPENHEIMER

Did you hear housing starts fell one percent today?

Most of it came from Bridgeport.

IBID.

POLAR BEAR KILLS A CHILD AT PROSPECT PARK ZOO

***New York Times,* May 20, 1987**

What do polar bears clean their teeth with?

Two spics

TRADER, FIRST BOSTON

Where did the little Puerto Rican kid say he was going?

To the maul

IBID.

What do you call a Puerto Rican kid who's been to the zoo?

Claude

IBID.

What did the polar bears say when the cops pulled up?

"What would you do if you found a Puerto Rican swimming in your pool?"

IBID.

Why did the police shoot the second polar bear?

It screamed "Howard Beach."

IBID.

How can you spot a polar bear at a Puerto Rican funeral?

It has a toothpick in its mouth.

IBID.

DELTA AIRLINES CREW IN NEAR COLLISION TRIED TO COVER IT UP

***New York Times*, July 11, 1987**

Did you hear about Delta Airlines' New Frequent Survivor Program?

TRADER, MORGAN STANLEY

Model from Texas Is Slashed in Face with Razor Blade; Former Landlord Arrested
***New York Times,* June 6, 1986**

What's written on Marla Hanson's résumé?

Model-slash-actress

COMMODITIES BROKER,
MERRILL LYNCH

Mirror, Mirror on the Wall, Who's the Worst One of Them All?

Wall Street's dark humor has generally been aimed outside of its own arena, but that all changed last year when the financial industry was rocked by its own series of scandals. It began with the indictment of thirty-three-year-old investment banker Dennis Levine in 1986 on insider-trading charges. Levine was charged by the government for illegally using knowledge of pending stock transactions to earn profits for himself. Since then, more than seventy prominent brokers and investment bankers have left their Wall Street district offices in handcuffs. Things got so bad that a top man at Morgan Stanley got on the firm's intercom one day with this query:

What's the difference between a Wall Streeter and a pig?

Not even a pig would stoop so low.

Wall Streeters have found even more good reasons to laugh at themselves, even when it hits their own profits. When Howard Rubin, a young trader at Merrill Lynch, gambled with the firm's money, contributing to the firm's $250 million loss, the first jokes came from the Merrill Lynch trading room:

What's the most expensive sandwich on Wall Street?
A Howard Rubin

What's the difference between a bond and a bond trader?
A bond matures.

FROM VARIOUS SOURCES

What do brokers say to their customers when they don't buy stock?
"Excuses are like assholes. Everyone has one and they all stink."

IBID.

Hear about the latest Merrill bid?
I bid one hundred Howies.

IBID.

Did you hear what they are changing the name of Bank of America to?
Insecurity Pacific

IBID.

Where is Dennis Levine vacationing?
Club Fed

IBID.

What does UJA stand for?
Unindicted Jewish Arb

IBID.

The Irish sing in pubs, the Italians sing at the opera. Where do Jews sing?
At the Securities and Exchange Commission

IBID.

You've heard of Live Aid, Farm Aid, now there's Arb Aid.

IBID.

What kind of bonds besides junk is Drexel Burnham Lambert now specializing in?
Bail bonds

IBID.

Hear about Drexel's latest drink?
Subpoena colada

IBID.

Did you hear about the new Drexel bond?
The maturity is twenty to life.

IBID.

What's the new Jefferies motto?
"Why buy stock when you can rent it?"

IBID.

What's Goldman Sachs' new name after Sumitomo Bank bought a stake in it?
Goldman Saki

IBID.

Knock, knock.
Who's there.
Ivan.
Ivan Who?
I've been taping our conversations.
Or
I've been talking to the Securities and Exchange Commission.

IBID.

A Wall Street lawyer, a doctor, and an architect are stranded on a desert island with no food, although across a shark-filled channel lies an island with lush coconut trees. The architect volunteers to swim across the channel for food, but as soon as he steps into the water, he's surrounded by sharks threatening his life. When he jumps out, the doctor says he'll try to swim across the channel for food. But the same thing happens.

"Well, it's up to me," says the lawyer, who dives in. This time the sharks part for him and let him swim to the island, where he picks some coconuts. He dives back into the channel, the sharks once again parting, and returns to the doctor and architect, who can't understand why he succeeded in getting food.

"Why did the sharks part for you?" asks the architect.

The lawyer shrugs and says, "Professional courtesy."

IBID.

Wall Streeters on Marriage

A construction worker goes into a bar and says he's having problems with his sex life. He turns to his black friend, Bubba, who advises: "When you go home tonight, set your lunch pail down loudly and bang your dick up against the screen door three times. Then take your wife and bang her in front of the refrigerator."

So the guy goes home and follows directions. Just as he's finishing with the screen door, his wife hollers: "Is that you, Bubba?"

FLOOR RUNNER, COMEX

A guy walks into his bedroom and finds his wife in bed with a midget.

"I thought you were going to put an end to this fooling around, dear," he exclaims.

"I am," she replies. "Can't you see I'm tapering off?"

FROM VARIOUS SOURCES

A man and a women are on their wedding night and after they make love, he asks her if she's hungry and wants to order room service. "My past lover was Jack Nicklaus, and he wouldn't do that. He'd keep making love," she says. So her husband resumes his lovemaking.

Six hours later, he says he's hungry and asks her if she wants room service yet. "Jack Nicklaus wouldn't do that. He'd keep making love to me," she declares. So her husband goes back to her. A little later, he asks again if she's hungry and she refuses.

"Do you have Jack's telephone number?" he asks.

"No, why?"

"I need to know what par is for this hole."

BARTENDER, FLUTIES

What's the definition of a wife?

An attachment a husband screws on a bed to get the housework done

FROM VARIOUS SOURCES

Why do Jewish husbands die before their wives?

Because they want to

TRADER, MORGAN STANLEY

What does a Polish groom give his bride that's long and hard?

His last name

BROKER, BEAR STEARNS

A guy goes into a bar and tells the bartender that he's upset. "Give me a shot of rye," he orders.

"But you're a beer drinker," the bartender protests.

"I just found out my kid is queer," the guy replies.

The next day, the same guy comes in and says, "Give me two shots of rye."

"Another bad day?" asks the bartender.

"I just found out both my kids are queer," the guy answers.

The day after that, the same guy returns and orders a whole bottle of rye.

"Doesn't anyone in your family eat pussy?" asks the bartender.

"I just found out my wife does," the guy replies.

FROM VARIOUS SOURCES

Wall Street on The Wide World of Sports

A guy goes to heaven and asks if there are any golf courses.

"Why yes," says an angel at the gate. "Over there."

So the guy wanders over to watch two men, one of whom he recognizes as St. Peter, playing in the mid-fairway. St. Peter takes out a seven iron and the other a five iron.

"Don't you think you better use another club?" asks St. Peter.

"No," says the other. "I saw Jack Nicklaus use a five-iron on this hole."

St. Peter hits the ball, and it lands on the green. The other guy hits the ball, and when it lands in a sandtrap, takes out a nine iron.

"Don't you think you better use your sand wedge?" asks St. Peter.

"No," the other guy answers. "I saw Jack Nicklaus use a nine iron in this trap." So he hits the ball and it lands on a lake off the green.

The observer watches incredulously as the guy walks on the water to find his golf ball. "Who does he think he is—Jesus?" the startled man asks St. Peter.

"Oh, he *is* Jesus, St. Peter responds. "But he *thinks* he's Jack Nicklaus."

BARTENDER, FLUTIES

What do seven-foot basketball players do in the off-season?

Go to the movies and sit in front of you

FROM VARIOUS SOURCES

Why are the Rams changing their names to the Tampons?

They are only good for one period and they have no second string.

IBID.

What do Michael Jackson and the Dodgers have in common?

They both wear one glove for no apparent reason.

IBID.

What kind of car does Renee Richards drive?

A convertible

IBID.

What's small, white and sells for two thousand dollars?

Dwight Gooden's rosin bag

IBID.

Did you hear that I sold Dwight Gooden's rookie card?

I got two grams.

IBID.

Why did the Chicago Bears want to recruit Dwight Gooden?

They wanted to put a coke machine next to the Refrigerator.

IBID.

Did you hear what the umpire yelled when the pitcher walked Dwight Gooden?

"Free base"

IBID.

Did you hear the Polish hockey team drowned?

Spring training

IBID.

Did you hear about the Pole who lost fifty dollars on the football game?

Twenty-five dollars on the game, and twenty-five dollars on the instant replay

IBID.

Did you hear Bill Buckner tried to commit suicide?

He jumped out in front of a bus and it went through his legs.

IBID.

Did you hear about the Pole who won the gold medal at the Olympics?

He had it bronzed.

IBID.

Why do they play on artificial turf in Poland?

To keep the cheerleaders from grazing

IBID.

Did you hear why the NFL is going to use green footballs next year.

A black never drops a watermelon.

IBID.

What's the definition of endless love?

Ray Charles and Stevie Wonder playing tennis

IBID.

Why did God invent golf?

So white people would have an excuse to get dressed up like black people

IBID.

What do they call a white athlete?

A Cokacian

IBID.

What do you get when you cross a black and a groundhog?

Six more weeks before basketball season

IBID.

What do a rose and Len Bias have in common?

Both died two days after they were picked.

IBID.

Sexchange: Brokers on Nature's Way

What's the difference between mono and herpes?

The difference is: you get mono from snatching a kiss.

TRADER, MORGAN STANLEY

Why is sex like a good bridge game?

You don't need a partner if you have a good hand.

IBID.

Did you hear about the man who got his vasectomy at Sears?

Every time the man has a hard-on, the garage door opens up.

IBID.

How do you know when you have an overbite?

When you're eating pussy and it tastes like shit

BARTENDER, McANN'S

How do you make paper dolls?
Screw an old bag.

IBID.

How can you tell a head nurse?
She's the one with dirty knees.

IBID.

What's the difference betwen oooh and aaah?
About six inches

MAILROOM, MERRILL LYNCH

Did you hear about the new designer condoms?
"Sergio Prevente"

TRADER, FIRST BOSTON

What do you call this? (puff cheeks out)
Polish sperm bank

ARBITRAGEUR, E.F. HUTTON

A Polish couple are in bed and things are heating up. The wife turns to her husband and says: "Take the hardest thing you've got and stick it where I pee." So her husband gets up, picks up his bowling ball, and throws it in the sink.

BROKER, DEAN WITTER REYNOLDS

What do you do when you come across an elephant?
You wipe it off.

IBID.

Why did the guy name his dog Herpes?

Because he wouldn't heel

IBID.

How do you know when two elephants have been screwing in your garage?

Because your Hefty Bags are missing

IBID.

Why do they call camels the ships of the desert?

Because they are full of Iranian semen

IBID.

Have you heard about the wallet made out of elephant foreskin?

Rub it and it becomes a suitcase.

INSTITUTIONAL SALES DESK,
SALOMON BROTHERS

What do a wildcat and a condom with a hole in it have in common?

You don't want to fuck with either one of them.

IBID.

Why is it a drag to screw a cow?

You have to climb down from the stump and walk around to the front every time you want to kiss her.

TRADER, KIDDER, PEABODY

Why don't blacks like blowjobs?
They don't like any jobs.

IBID.

Why do blacks always have sex on their minds?
Because of the pubic hair on their heads

IBID.

Why are Jewish men circumcised?
Jewish women won't buy anything unless it's twenty percent off.

COMMODITIES BROKER, E. DAVID STEPHENS

What's the difference between a circumcision and crucifixion?
In a crucifixion, they throw out the whole Jew.

IBID.

Define Jewish foreplay.
Two hours of begging

IBID.

What's the definition of black foreplay?
"Don't scream or I'll kill you."

FLOOR RUNNER,
AMERICAN STOCK EXCHANGE

What's Italian foreplay?
"Hey yo, you awake?"

IBID.

What's Polish foreplay?
ZZZZZZZ (snore)

IBID.

What do lesbians need to get married?
A licker license

INSTITUTIONAL SALES DESK, MERRILL LYNCH

What's the difference between a pervert and a kinky person?
The pervert uses a feather and the kinky person uses the whole chicken.

IBID.

Did you hear Ben-Hur had a sex change?
Now he's Ben-Gay.

BARTENDER, FLUTIES

Why did God make urine yellow and come white?
So Italians could tell if they were coming or going

BROKER, MKI MONEY MARKETS

What's the definition of a maniac?
An Italian in a whorehouse with a credit card

IBID.

Why do Polish men make such lousy lovers?
Because they always wait for the swelling to go down

IBID.

Wall Street on Women

Forget everything you've ever heard about women's lib on Wall Street. Men still dominate most of the positions on the Street, and the conventional male attitudes toward women and sex are pretty pervasive. In fact, only a few women on Wall Street contributed any jokes to this book, and only one of those jokes is similar in style to those in this section:

Why did God create man?
Because he couldn't teach a vibrator to mow a lawn

What's the definition of a woman?
Life support for a pussy

TRADER, COMEX

Why do women have two holes so close together?
So you can carry them home like a six-pack

FLOOR RUNNER, AMEX

Why did God invent women?
Because sheep can't cook

BARTENDER, McANN'S

What's the definition of the perfect woman?

◇ *She's three feet tall, has a round hole for a mouth, her head is flat to put cocktails on, and she has two horns to grab on to.*
◇ *The sports model has pull-back ears and her teeth fold in.*
◇ *The economy model fucks all night and at midnight turns into a roast-beef sandwich and a six-pack.*

INVESTMENT BANKER, BANKERS TRUST

A guy walks into a bar, goes up to the bartender, and says, "Give me a scotch and soda, and I'd like to buy that douche bag at the end of the bar a drink."

The bartender exclaims, "Hey, she's a regular and you can't be talking about her like that."

The guy agrees. "Okay, then I'd like to buy that nice lady at the end of the bar a drink."

When the bartender asks her what she wants, she replies, "Vinegar and water."

FLOOR RUNNER, AMEX

Why are cowgirls bowlegged?
Because cowboys like to eat with their hats on

BROKER, E.F. HUTTON

Why do women have two holes so close together?
In case a man misses

IBID.

What two things in the air can make a woman pregnant?

Her legs

SECRETARY, PRUDENTIAL-BACHE

What's the definition of virginity?

A big issue over a little tissue

BROKER, D.H. BLAIR

Why do women rub their eyes in the morning when they get up?

Because they don't have balls to scratch

TRADER, FIRST BOSTON

Why does a female paratrooper wear a jockstrap when she parachutes?

So she doesn't whistle on the way down

TRADER, AMEX

What's organic dental floss?

Pubic hair

BROKER, D.H. BLAIR

An investment bank asks three female job candidates the following question: "If you found an extra ten thousand dollars added by mistake to your paycheck, what would you do?"

The first says, "Give it back."

The second says, "Keep it."

The third says, "Split it."

Which one did they hire?

The one with the biggest tits

INVESTMENT BANKER, PAINEWEBBER

How many men does it take to clean an office?
None. It's a woman's job.

IBID.

What's approximately six inches long, has a head on it, and women love it?
A dollar bill

COMMODITIES BROKER, COMEX

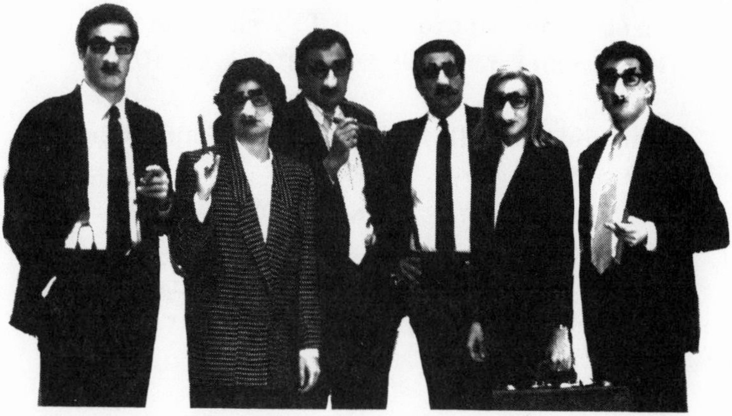

A girl is out on the golf course for the first time, and gets stung by a bee. She runs back to the golf pro to tell him.

"Where?" he asks.

"Between the first and second hole," she replies.

"You have to close your stance a little."

BARTENDER, FLUTIES

Why did God make woman after man?
He didn't want any advice.

IBID.

A woman goes to the doctor to complain about her knees. The doctor asks her about the source of her stress. Does she jog? No, she says. Does she do aerobics? No, she says. "Then I don't know what's wrong," remarks the puzzled doctor. "Just what do you do on your knees?"

The woman pauses and says, "Well, I'm on all fours when I have sex with my husband."

"There are other positions," the doctor informs her.

"Not if you want to watch TV," she replies.

ANALYST, NEW YORK STOCK EXCHANGE

Why did the Valley Girl wear two diaphragms?

For sure, for sure

BROKER, MORGAN STANLEY

Why do women have trouble telling distances?

All their lives, they're told, "This is six inches."

IBID.

Why are a moped and a fat lady similar?

They're both fun to ride, but you don't want your friends to see you on either one.

IBID.

Why do Mexican women wear long skirts?

To hide the No-Pest strip

BROKER, MONTGOMERY SECURITIES

Did you hear about the Polish lesbian?

She loved men.

RESEARCH ASSISTANT, OPPENHEIMER

What do Polish women do when they're through sucking a cock?

They spit out the feathers.

BARTENDER, McANN'S

What's the most useless thing on a Polish woman's body?

A Polish man

IBID.

What's the difference between a Polish girl and a bowling ball?

If you had to, you could eat a bowling ball.

IBID.

How do you know when a Polish girl is menstruating?

She's only wearing one sock.

BROKER, MKI MONEY MARKETS

What do you call a Polish girl with half a brain?

Gifted

IBID.

What do you call a beautiful girl in Poland?

A tourist

BROKER, MERRILL LYNCH

Why don't Polish women like vibrators?

Because they chip their teeth

IBID.

A young Polish girl walks into a sperm bank, and the nurse there asks, "Can I help you?"

"Yes," she replies. "Where do you want me to spit this stuff?"

BROKER, MKI MONEY MARKETS

Where can you buy panties made out of fertilizer bags and bras made out of beer cans?

Frederick's of Poland

BROKER, MERRILL LYNCH

What do you call a black lady with braces?

A Black & Decker Pecker Wrecker

TRADER, FIRST BOSTON

Who are the two most famous black women in history?

Aunt Jemima and Motha Fucker

IBID.

What do you call a black woman in the army?

A Waccoon

COMMODITIES BROKER, COMEX

What did the Valley Girl say after having oral sex with a black man?

"Gag me with a coon."

TRADER, MORGAN STANLEY

What do you get when you cross a Jewish American Princess with a computer?

A computer that never goes down on you

IBID.

What's a JAP's favorite wine?

*"I wanna go to Miami [*or *Palm Springs;* or *shopping]."*

IBID.

What's the difference between JAPs and Jell-O?

Jell-O moves when you eat it.

INVESTMENT ADVISOR, J.W. GANT & ASSOCIATES

How does a JAP do it doggy-style?

She makes him beg for an hour.

IBID.

What do you call a Jewish woman's waterbed?

The Dead Sea

IBID.

What's the difference between a JAP and a vulture?

A vulture waits until you're dead to eat your heart out.

IBID.

What's a JAP's favorite position?
Facing Bloomingdale's

BROKER, MORGAN STANLEY

What's a JAP's idea of natural childbirth?
Absolutely no makeup

IBID.

Why do JAPs close their eyes while screaming?
So they can pretend they're shopping

IBID.

What's a JAP's idea of perfect sex?
Simultaneous headaches

IBID.

How do you know when a JAP is having an orgasm?
She drops her nail file.

IBID.

What does a Jewish woman say to her kids before dinner?
"Get in the car."

IBID.

What do you call five thousand Jewish woman in front of Bloomingdale's waiting for the store to open for the Columbus Day sale?
Yidlock

BROKER, DEAN WITTER REYNOLDS

How do you know when you're making love to a prostitute, a nymphomaniac, or a JAP?

By her comment when you're finished.

The prostitute says, "That's it."

The nympho asks, "That's it?"

The JAP says, "Peach... the ceiling should be peach."

IBID.

How many JAPs does it take to screw in a light bulb?

Two. One to get the Diet Pepsi and the other to call Daddy.

IBID.

How many Jewish mothers does it take to screw in a light bulb?

Zero. "That's okay, I'll sit here in the dark."

IBID.

What do JAPs make for dinner?

Reservations

IBID.

How do you cure a JAP of nymphomania?

Marry her.

IBID.

What do you call twenty JAPs in your basement?

The whinecellar

IBID.

Did you hear about the Italian girl who thought a sanitary belt was a drink from a clean shot glass?

BROKER, FUTURES EXCHANGE

Why are Italian mothers square-shouldered?
From raising dumbbells

IBID.

Who won the Italian beauty contest?
No one

IBID.

What do spaghetti and women have in common?
They both wiggle when you eat them.

IBID.

Wall Street's Bathroom Humor

Bad taste and bad humor seem to go hand in hand on Wall Street. But the same tasteless jokes are told over and over again. Most seem funnier after a few beers, but then again, what isn't?

Why are eggs so frustrated?

Because they only get laid once, they only get eaten once, they only get beaten once, and you've gotta boil them to get them hard

INVESTMENT MANAGER, BANKERS TRUST

How do you get a Kleenex to dance?

Blow a little boogie into it.

BROKER, D.H. BLAIR

Why is there a string at the end of a tampon?

So you can floss after you eat

TRADER, E.F. HUTTON

One ovary says to the other ovary, "Hey, did you order any furniture?"

The second ovary says: "No, why?"

"There's a couple of nuts outside trying to shove an organ in."

BANKER, CHEMICAL BANK

Why do women have more trouble with hemorrhoids than men?

Because God made man the perfect asshole

IBID.

Have you heard about the new deodorant called "Umpire"?

It's for foul balls.

IBID.

What's brown and sounds like a doorbell?

Dung

FLOOR RUNNER, COMEX

Why don't pygmies wear tampons?

They keep stepping on the string.

IBID.

Why is pubic hair curly?

If it were straight, it would poke your eyes out.

IBID.

Why do farts smell?

So deaf people can appreciate them too

IBID.

How can you tell if a woman is wearing panty hose?
If her ankles swell up when she farts

IBID.

What's the last thing that goes through a bug's mind as it hits your windshield?
Its asshole

BROKER, MONTGOMERY SECURITIES

What's the fourth biggest lie?
It's only a cold sore.

TRADER, FIRST BOSTON

Why aren't cowboys circumcised?
So they have someplace to keep their Skoal while they're eating

BANKER, CITIBANK

What's blue and comes in Brownies?
Cub Scouts

IBID.

Do you know the main difference between a cheeseburger and a blowjob?
You want to go to lunch?

TRADER, MORGAN STANLEY

Ever smell mothballs?
How did you get their legs apart?

BARTENDER, FLUTIES

There are two brokers, one from Harvard and the other from Yale, in the bathroom. One says to the other, "At Yale, they teach us to wash our hands after we piss."

The other replies, "At Harvard, they teach us not to piss in our hands."

BROKER, MKI MONEY MARKETS

Why can't you circumcise an Iranian?
Because there's no end to those pricks.

IBID.

What has a thousand teeth and eats wienies?
A zipper

IBID.

What do you call a truckload of vibrators?
Toys for twats

IBID.

What can you use tampons for?
Tea bags for vampires

BROKER, DEAN WITTER REYNOLDS

What's red and has seven dents?
Snow White's cherry

IBID.

What do beans and dildos have in common?
Both are meat substitutes.

IBID.

Have you heard about Procter & Gamble's new product?

Toxic shock absorbers

TRADER, FIRST BOSTON

Have you heard of the new Tox Shock rock group?

They only play ragtime.

BROKER, SMITH BARNEY

What do you get when you mix holy water with castor oil?

A religious movement

RESEARCH ANALYST, OPPENHEIMER

What were the first words Adam spoke to Eve?

"Stand back. I don't know how big this thing gets."

BROKER, D.H. BLAIR

What's the best thing to give an eighty-year-old woman?

Mikey, because he'll eat anything

IBID.

What's brown and soft and sits on a piano bench?

Beethoven's First Movement

IBID.

OVERHEARD IN THE MAIL ROOM

How do you circumcise a whale?

Send down four skin divers.

What do you get when you cross a donkey with an onion?

An ass that will bring tears to your eyes

What do you call a cow that plays with itself?

Beef Strokenoff

What do you call a cow with an abortion?

Decalfinated

Why do gorillas have such big nostrils?

Because their fingers are so big

What do you get when you cross a rooster with peanut butter?

A cock that sticks to the roof of your mouth

What do Tupperware and a walrus have in common?

They both like a tight seal.

What's big and white and lives on the ocean floor?

The Ku Klux Clam

Where do you get virgin wool?

From ugly sheep

Why are chickens so ugly?

You'd be ugly too if you had a pecker hanging out of your forehead.

What's the brown stuff between an elephant's toes?
Slow natives

What do you have when there are one hundred rabbits standing in a row and they are hopping backwards?
A receding hareline

BEAR MARKET, OR JOKES FOR A SLOW AFTERNOON

Wall Street generally operates at a rocketlike pace. And most people there like its hyperactivity. A slow day is rare, and occurs particularly during the last two weeks of August, when the rest of the world is on vacation. It's a time when the phone doesn't ring as frequently, leaving fewer deals to do and less business to generate. And time to make up some more complex jokes, quips, and puns. Here are some favorites, all from various sources.

Why is San Francisco like granola?
Because once you get past the fruits and nuts, all you have left is the flakes.

Did you hear about the queer nail?
It was laid in the road and blew a tire.

Did you hear about the deaf gynecologist?
He had to learn how to read lips.

What's better than roses on your piano?
Tulips on your organ

Why was time-out called in the leper hockey game?
There was a face-off in the corner.

Two seventy-five-year-old women, Sadie and Mildred, go to the beach to celebrate their birthdays. There, they spot two ninety-five-year-old men, Sam and Saul, taking a walk.

"Let's streak," says Sadie.

As they run by naked, Sam, in shock, says, "What's that?"

"I don't know," says Saul. "But it sure needs ironing."

Why don't Puerto Ricans have checking accounts?
Because it's hard to sign checks with a spray can.

What does a man do standing up, a woman sitting down, and a dog on three legs?
Shake hands

What do you call a Philippine contortionist?
A Manila folder

How can you tell if you have bad acne?
If a blind man reads your face

What's black and red and has a hard time getting through a revolving door?
A nun with a spear in her head

What do you call kids born in whorehouses?
Brothel sprouts

What do you call a midget psychic who just committed a crime?
A small medium at large

What's green and makes holes?
A drill pickle

What has orange hair, big feet, and comes out of a test tube?
Bozo the Clone

What's the good thing about having Alzheimer's disease?
You meet a new person every day.

What's the yuppie solution to illness?
Starve a cold, cater a fever

Why can't blind people skydive?
It scares the shit out of their dogs.

What's the difference between a moose and Guy Lombardo's orchestra?
With a moose, the horns are in the front and the asshole is in the rear.

Why haven't they cremated Colonel Sanders yet?
They haven't decided whether to do him regular or extra-crispy.

Write down the Jewish New Year: 5748.
Write down the Chinese New Year: 4686.
Now subtract: The difference is 1,062. What's that?
The number of years Jews went without Chinese food

What're the five most common words said to a black man in a three-piece suit?
"Will the defendant please rise?"

Have you heard about the Jewish porn film?
It's called Debbie Does Nothing.

Place your hand out, palm parallel to the floor, and dangle the third finger, keeping other fingers stretched flat. What's that?
Superman flying over a nudist colony

What do you call this? (Stick tongue out)
A lesbian with a hard-on

Why was Christopher Columbus the best deal maker in history?
He left not knowing where he was going, and upon arriving, not knowing where he was. He returned not knowing where he had been. And he did it all on borrowed money.

Why did British ships come back from the Falklands full of sheep?
War brides

WALL STREET BROKERS' EXAM

SAND (boxed) 1.	MAN ——— BOARD 2.	/r/e/a/d/i/n/g 3.	STAND ——— I 4.
WEAR ——— LONG 5.	R ROADS A D S 5.	T O W N 7.	CYCLE CYCLE CYCLE 8.
LE VEL 9.	O ——— M.D. Ph.D. B.S. 10.	KNEE Lights 11.	IIII —— u 12.
Ċhair 13.	DICE DICE 14.	T O U C H 15.	GROUND ——— FEET FEET FEET FEET FEET 16. FEET
MIND ——— MATTER 17.	he's / himself 18.	E C N A L G 19.	DEATH / LIFE 20.
GI —— CCC CC C 21.	____ PROGRAM 22.	B L O U S E 23.	J YOU U ME S T 24.

EACH ANSWER WORTH 4 POINTS—TOTAL OF 100.

Answers on page 76.

What's worse than getting raped by Jack the Ripper?

Getting fingered by Captain Hook

What's black, crispy, and comes on a stick?

Joan of Arc

What do you get when you cross a stud with a debtor?

Someone who's always into you for at least ten inches

BULL MARKET, OR JOKES FOR A FAST DAY

Jokes are a way to warm up a customer when you have business to do. But the setup and answer better be quick and obvious, because the telephone will continue to ring. The point is to do the deal quickly and move on.

These are some of the favorites; they're too popular for me to credit any one author.

What do you call a man with no arms and no legs hanging on the wall?

Art

What do you call his arms and legs on the wall?

Pieces of Art

What do you call a man with no arms and no legs floating in the water?

Bob

What do you call a man with no arms and no legs in a pile of leaves?

Russell

What do you call a man with no arms and no legs in front of a door?

Matt

What do you call a man with no arms and no legs who has a speech impediment and is sitting in the bathtub?

Dwayne

What do you call a man with no arms and no legs sitting on a grill?

Frank

What do you call a woman with no arms and no legs sitting on a grill?

Patty

How do you keep a moron in suspense?

(Say nothing)

Have you heard about the new Oriental cookbook?

It's called 101 Ways to Wok Your Dog.

What do the post office and Kinney's have in common?

Both have thirty thousand black loafers.

Why don't Mexicans barbecue?

Because the beans slip through the grill

Why are black men moving to Houston?
Because there are no jobs there

What do you get when you cross a Japanese lady and a Chinese lady?
A broad who sucks laundry

What's a Greek gentleman?
A man who takes a girl out three times before he propositions her brother

Why does Helen Keller have yellow legs?
Because her dog is blind too

Why does Helen Keller masturbate with only one hand?
She needs the other to moan.

Did you hear about the new Helen Keller dolls?
Wind them up and they walk into walls.

What's the only kind of wood that doesn't float?
Natalie Wood

What's the last thing Natalie Wood's mother said to her?
"Have a couple of drinks, dear, but don't go overboard."

What do you call Santa Claus's helpers?
Subordinated clauses

APPLICATION FOR EMPLOYMENT
Simplified form for minority applicants

Black applicant: It is not necessary to attach a photograph, since you all look alike.
Mexican: List date of illegal entry into the United States.

Name:__________ __________ __________ __________
First Last Middle Alias

Address: ______________________________
If living in an automobile, give make, license, and where parked.

Name of Parents: Mother (1)________ Father: (1)________
(2)________ (2)________
(3)________ (3)________

Place of Birth: Charity Hospital ( ) Cotton Patch ( )
Empty Freight Car ( )

Marital Status: Common Lay ( ) Multiple ( ) Other ( )

Type of Vehicle: Lincoln ( ) Cadillac ( ) Rolls-Royce ( )
If Mexican, list name of pickup truck: ____________

Number of children claimed on Welfare: ____________
Number of legitimate children (if any): ____________

List approximate estimate of income and indicate sources:
$________Theft
$________Welfare
$________Unemployment

Check any machine that you can operate by yourself:
Telephone ( ) Television ( ) Coke Machine ( )
Wheelbarrow ( ) Slot Machine ( ) Washing Machine ( )

Work Experience: Tap Dancer ( ) Protest Leader ( )
Dope Pusher ( ) V.D. Spreader ( )
All of the above mentioned ( )

If applicant is Mexican: Lettuce Picker ( ) Tomato Picker ( )
Potato Picker ( )
Governor of Arizona ( )

Check food you like best:
Barbecue Ribs ( ) Tripe ( ) Watermelon ( ) Chitlins ( )

If Mexican: Rice ( ) Beans ( )
Rice and Beans ( ) Beans and Rice ( )

In fifty words or less, list your greatest desire in life (other than a white woman):
____
____
____
____

Mexican applicants may omit the above, if they don't know fifty (50) words.

How many psychiatrists does it take to change a light bulb?

None. It has to be willing to change itself.

How many Californians does it take to change a light bulb?

Five. One to screw it in and four to share the experience.

What's the definition of macho?

Running home after your vasectomy

Wall Street English Test

What do these have in common with Shakespeare?

WET DRY
MISCARRIAGE
4″ 8″ 12″

Answers:

Wet = *Midsummer Night's Dream*
Dry = *Twelfth Night*
Miscarriage = *Love's Labour's Lost*
4″ = *Much Ado About Nothing*
8″ = *As You Like It*
12″ = *The Taming of the Shrew*

AFTER-HOURS HUMOR

A Wall Streeter's day usually ends about 5 P.M. for brokers and traders, and later than that for bankers. There are several watering holes on Wall Street, though—Delmonico's, Harry's, Harry's at the American Stock Exchange, and a new addition, the South Street Seaport, where Wall Streeters unwind from the grueling pace and pressure of their jobs. These are the final jokes of the day, when a good anecdote is a way to mask a drop in the market or celebrate a new fortune.

What's the definition of mixed emotions?

Your mother-in-law going over a cliff in your new BMW

A guy goes into a bar and the bartender says, "Would you like an apple or a beer?"

"Why an apple?" the guy asks.

"It tastes like pussy," the bartender replies.

So the guy takes a bite out of the apple. "This tastes like shit!" he cries, spitting it out.

"That figures," says the bartender. "You bit the wrong end."

A housewife is at the supermarket checkout counter watching a handsome kid bag her groceries. She's horny and decides to make a play, so as they walk out to the parking lot, she says, "I have an itchy pussy."

"What color?" the kid asks. "All those Japanese cars look the same to me."

A guy goes into a whorehouse looking for some action. "I want the best," he tells the madam.

"The Yellow Hurricane is the best," she replies. "That will cost three hundred dollars."

The guy says, "That's a lot, but okay." So he goes upstairs to the room, finds a beautiful blond woman, undresses, and starts giving her some action.

As he gets excited, she blows into his ear. "What are you doing?" he asks.

"It's the wind in the hurricane," she tells him. So they keep at it and a little while later, she starts peeing.

"What's going on?" he asks.

"It's the rain in the hurricane," she explains. He mounts her again and now she starts farting. "That's the thunder of the hurricane," she says. He gets off her and starts dressing.

"Where are you going?" she asks.

"Honey, I can't fuck you in this weather."

An American businessman goes to Japan and rents a whore. As they start making it, she says something that sounds like *yakersony*. That must mean *good*, he thinks.

The next day he's out playing golf with some Japanese businessmen, and he gets a hole in one. "Yakersony!" he cries.

"Why did you say that?" asks one of the Japanese men. "It means *wrong hole*."

A guy picks up a girl in a bar and she agrees to go back to his apartment after she tells him something.

"What?" he asks.

"I have my menstrual cycle," she says.

"That's okay, just put it in the trunk," he replies.

A guy goes into a bar and asks the bartender about the atomic bomb. So the bartender asks, "Do you know what the difference is between rabbit and elephant feces?"

"No," the guy says.

"You want to talk about the atomic bomb, and you don't know your shit?"

A guy walks into a bar and orders three martinis. The bartender says, "You're having a good day."

The guy answers, "I'm celebrating my first blowjob."

The bartender says, "Let me buy you a fourth."

The buyer replies, "No, I think three should wash the taste out."

Two little kids are playing cards. In the first round, the little boy has two jacks and the little girl has two kings. In the second round, the little boy has three jacks and the little girl three aces. In the third round, the little boy has three aces and the little girl four kings. The little boy gets so frustrated that he pulls down his pants, points to his penis, and says, "Well, I have one of these."

She in turn takes down her pants and says, "Well, I have one of these."

And he says, "But you can never have one of these."

She replies, "Oh, yes I can. With one of these, I can have as many of those as I want."

There are two brokers, George and Lenny. Everyone knows Lenny, but not George. Everywhere they go, everyone says hello to Lenny. George becomes so frustrated, he thinks up a plan. "Lenny," he says one day, "I think I know one guy who doesn't know you." So they fly to Rome, where George announces, "We're going to the Vatican to see the pope."

Lenny laughs. "George, you're wrong. The pope and I are old friends." And he's right. The second the pope sees Lenny, he hugs and greets him, and the pope and Lenny go up to the papal balcony to wave to the crowds.

While George waits down in St. Peter's Square, someone comes up to him and says, "Hey, who's that with Lenny?"

There's a Russian ambassador and an African ambassador meeting for the first time at a cocktail party. "What kind of games do you play?" the African asks the Russian.

"Well," says the Russian, pulling him aside, "we have Russian roulette, where you take a gun with one bullet loaded in its cartridge and you point it to your head. You gamble that the next click won't be it. Want to try?"

"Sounds easy. Sure," says the African. They go to a back room where the Russian hands the African a pistol. He points it to his head, pulls the trigger, and there's no bullet. "Oh, that's nothing," he says to the Russian. "Come with me."

So the Russian follows him to the African embassy to a back room where there are seven naked women kneeling with their mouths open. "Now," says the African, "put your dick in one of their mouths."

The Russian unzips his pants. "So what's the game?" he asks, looking over the women.

"One's a cannibal," says the African.

A guy is crawling in the desert, dying of thirst. First, he sees a man, and asks for water. "No," says the man. "I have no water, but I can give you a shirt."

The man refuses the shirt and keeps crawling. Not soon after, he comes across another man. "I need water," he begs.

"I have no water," the man says, "but I have a necktie."

The guy refuses and keeps crawling. After several hours, he comes upon an oasis, but it is barred by a guard and a gate. "Let me in," he begs the guard.

The guard looks him over. "Sorry, sir," he says. "Shirt and necktie are required."

A heroic cowboy defeats an Indian tribe and the chief invites him to his tepee after the battle. "I'm awarding you three wishes. All you have to do is whisper your wish into my magic horse's ear and he will grant your desire."

So the cowboy goes over to the horse and whispers in its ear. Soon after, the horse comes back with a beautiful brunette squaw. "You are satisfied?" asks the chief. The cowboy shakes his head, and whispers something else into the horse's ear. Soon after, the horse comes back with a blond squaw. "You are satisfied?" the chief asks again. The cowboy shakes his head. "Maybe you should speak louder. My horse may be getting hard of hearing," the chief suggests.

"*Posse*!" the cowboy screams at the horse. "I said *posse*."

Answers to Brokers' Exam (page 65)

1. *sandbox*
2. *man overboard*
3. *reading between the lines*
4. *I understand*
5. *long underwear*
6. *crossroads*
7. *downtown*
8. *tricycle*
9. *split level*
10. *3 degrees below zero*
11. *neon lights*
12. *eyes on you*
13. *high chair*
14. *pair of dice*
15. *touchdown*
16. *dead (six feet underground)*
17. *mind over matter*
18. *he's beside himself*
19. *backward glance*
20. *life after death*
21. *GI overseas*
22. *space program*
23. *see-through blouse*
24. *just between you and me*

Sex, Drugs, and Rock 'n' Roll: Wall Street on Hollywood, Washington, and the Afterlife

It's a rare time when scandal seems pervasive, but that's been the case recently. Wall Street's own insider-trading scam was matched by the AIDS scare in Hollywood, Gary Hart's gaffe over Donna Rice in Washington, and TV evangelist Jim Bakker's scandalous embroilment with Jessica Hahn. While Wall Street has always been cynical about these other power centers (and that includes heaven), recent events have provided fresh material for satire. And the biting commentary of these jokes has a darker side: "It's a time of fallen idols," said one banker. Yet there's no conspiracy. Malcolm Forbes, Madonna, and Bill Cosby have not been implicated.

So many people told me these, I can't possibly give any one person credit.

WHAT INQUIRING WALL STREET MINDS LIKE TO KNOW

How do they say "Fuck you" in Los Angeles?

"Trust me."

Have you heard about the new Mexican disaster movie?

It's called Tacolipsnow.

Have you heard about the new war movie they're making with an all-black cast?

It's called Apackoflips Now.

What do Loretta Swit and Richard Pryor have in common?

They've both had Major Burns on their face.

Did you hear about the new movie Mel Brooks is producing starring Michael Jackson and Richard Pryor?

It's called Blazing Sambos.

What would Princess Grace be doing if she were alive today?

Scratching on the lid of her coffin

Who taught Princess Grace how to drive?

Teddy Kennedy

What song did they play at Princess Grace's funeral?

"She'll be Comin' Round the Mountain When She Comes"

What's blue and sings alone?

Dan Aykroyd

Why does Dolly Parton have such a small waist?

Nothing grows in the shade.

What do you call the sweat between Dolly Parton's tits?

Mountain Dew

How can you pick Dolly Parton's kids in a crowd?

They're the ones with stretch marks around their mouths.

Why does Dolly Parton shop at Nissan for her bras?
They're the only company with a 280Z.

Do you think John Belushi would be alive today if he said, "No Coke, Pepsi"?

What was Dino Martin Jr.'s last hit?
The mountain

What's Dino Martin Jr.'s theme song?
"All of Me Everywhere at Once"

What do Marvin Gaye and his records have in common?
Both are black with holes in the middle.

Why did Rock Hudson date a black man?
He wanted to put some color in his cheeks.

What do Liberace and the Staten Island Ferry have in common?
Both went bobbing on the Hudson.

How did AIDS get to New York City?
Up the Hudson

What do Rock Hudson and Donald Manes have in common?
Both screwed queens.

What do Richard Pryor and Rock Hudson have in common?

Both got a little bit of bad crack

What did Rock Hudson ask when semen rose to the top of the hot tub he was sharing with Liberace and Boy George?

"Who farted?"

Why did Rock Hudson's lover get mad at him?

Because he came home shit-faced

Who's the most nervous actress in Hollywood?

The last to get a piece of the Rock

Why did they bury Liberace face down?

◊ *So his friends would recognize him*

◊ *So his friends could have a cold one*

Did you hear Liberace didn't really have AIDS?

The guy behind him did.

The Monday before Liberace's death, why did his friends predict he'd live six more weeks?

A gerbil crawled out of his ass and saw his shadow.

Did you hear Liberace felt a little better the night before he died?

He got up on his knees.

Why did Liberace have so many candelabras?

So his friends would have somewhere to sit

Did you hear Liberace didn't really die of AIDS?
He died of botulism: bad meat in a can.

What did they write on Liberace's tombstone?
"Ashes to ashes, dust to dust, if he'd been into women, he'd still be with us."

What was the toast at Liberace's wake?
"Bottom's up"

What does AIDS stand for?
Adios, Infected Dick Sucker

What did they find when they performed an autopsy on Liberace?
Michael Jackson's other glove

One broker to another broker: "I have good news and bad news. The good news is that they found Liberace's wallet. The bad news is your picture is in it."

Did you hear that Liberace wanted to buy the Baltimore Colts?
He heard that they had one tight end and that they all sucked.

What's Liberace doing now?
Decomposing

What's the real reason why Liberace got AIDS?

◊ *He was great on the piano, bad on the organ.*

◊ *He forgot to wash his organ after so many hymns.*

What goes into thirteen twice?

Roman Polanski

Why did Maria Shriver really marry Arnold Schwarzenegger?

To produce a race of bullet-proof candidates.

What did Vanna White say when asked her favorite consonants?

"North America and South America."

EARS OVER THE POTOMAC

How is Ronald Reagan like an IBM Selectric?

Both have a short-term memory.

What's the difference between Rock Hudson and Ronald Reagan?

Reagan's aides haven't killed him yet.

What do Gary Hart and Prime Minister Nakasone have in common?

Both eat rice.

Ronnie and Nancy Reagan go out to a restaurant for a nice dinner. "What would you like, madam?" the waiter asks Nancy.

"I'll have the fish filet," she replies.

"And for the vegetable?" the waiter asks.

"Oh, he'll have the same," she says.

Hart, Ted Kennedy, and Nixon are on a boat that starts to sink. Concerned about the others, Kennedy demands that the lifeboats be filled. "Women first," he yells.

Nixon replies, "Fuck the women."

"There isn't time," says Hart.

What's the biggest mistake Gary Hart made?

That he didn't ask Teddy Kennedy to drive Donna Rice home

What does Teddy Kennedy always say?

"We'll drive over that bridge when we come to it."

What's Gary Hart's new campaign slogan?

"I'm after Bush."

How does Gary Hart talk to his wife during sex?

On the telephone

Did you hear what Gary Hart did about the abortion bill?

He paid it.

Did you hear about the Gary Hart diet?

The Rice Diet

Did you hear about the new law firm Richard Nixon, Gary Hart, and Teddy Kennedy formed?

It's called Trick 'em, Dick 'em, and Dunk 'em.

What do Donna Rice and Christa McAuliffe have in common?

◊ *Both went down on a challenger.*

◊ *Both got blown off the state of Florida.*

Did you hear Donna Rice really didn't ride in the *Monkey Business*?

She was on Gary Hart's dinghy.

What is the difference between Donna Rice and Christa McAuliffe?

One blew apart; one blew a Hart.

What did Prime Minister Nakasone say to Gary Hart?

"Good ruck on your next erection."

What did Jim Brady say when he was asked how he felt about his job?

◊ *"I must have had a hole in my head to take this job."*

◊ *"If I had half a brain, I'd leave."*

WHY HEAVEN CAN WAIT

What's the name of Jim Bakker's thirteen naked women?

A Bakker's dozen

What does PTL stand for?

Pay The Lady

What's soft and white and cost $225,000?

Jim Bakker's pecker

If you added another K to Jim Bakker's name, what would have happened?

He'd have been caught under the sheet, instead of on top.

Did you hear where they found Jimmy Hoffa?

Under Tammy Bakker's makeup

Four nuns go to their local parish for confession. The first goes into the confessional booth and says: "Father I have sinned. My finger accidentally touched a man's testicles."

The priest replied: "Say four Hail Marys and, on your way out, dip that finger into the font of holy water."

She does, and the second nun goes into the confessional and says: "Father, I have sinned. My hand accidentally brushed up against a man's penis."

The priest replies: "Say four Hail Marys and, on your way out, submerge that hand in the font of holy water."

The fourth nun has been watching all of this and says to the third: "Do you mind if I go next? I want to gargle in the holy water before you sit in it."

BROKER, MKI MONEY MARKETS

There's a Catholic priest, a Methodist minister, and a Jewish rabbi talking about divvying up the money taken for collection for either charity or the individual parish. The Catholic priest says: "In our church, we draw a line down the middle, throw the collection plate full of money in the air, and the money that lands on the right side of the line goes to charity and to the left of the line, our church."

The Methodist minister says: "In our church, we draw a circle and throw the money into the air, and what lands outside the circle, we keep for our church and give the rest to charity."

The Jewish rabbi says: "We just throw the money in the air and wait for the hand of God. What he doesn't take, we keep."

IBID.

Did you hear Easter was canceled?
They found the body.

This guy named O'Leary had a dog for seventeen years. One day it passes away and O'Leary is so upset that he goes to his local parish and asks Father Moran: "My dog passed away. Will you give me a good Christian burial?"

The priest looks stunned and says, "We don't do that kind of thing here. But a guy down the road will do it for four hundred dollars."

O'Leary says, "Well, I planned to spend at least four thousand dollars."

Father Moran replies, "Of course I'll do it. You never told me it was a Catholic dog."

Why wasn't Christ born in Italy?
Because they couldn't find three wise men and a virgin

Why is a synagogue round?
So Jews can't hide in corners when the collection plate comes around

Frederick Busch, the Milwaukee beer baron of Anheuser-Busch fame, was a devout Catholic all of his life. In his later years, in declining health, he requested an audience with the pope.

After being ushered into the pontiff's presence and spending a few minutes on the social amenities, he said, "Your Holiness, do you know the line from the Lord's prayer, 'Give us this day, our daily bread'?"

"Yes, my son, of course."

"Well, Your Holiness, I'm willing to make a donation to the Church of $100,000 if you would be willing to change it to 'Give us this day our daily beer.' "

Somewhat taken aback, the pope replied: "I'm sorry, my son, but that's out of the question."

"Your Holiness, I'd be willing to increase my contribution to $250,000 if you would change it."

"That's most generous, my son, but you don't realize what you're asking. I'm afraid that would be impossible."

Once more, Busch tried. "I would be willing to give you half a million dollars if you could just change that one word."

"I'm overwhelmed my son, but it simply cannot be done."

So Busch thanked His Holiness and left the room.

The pope sat for a minute, deep in thought, and then picked up the telephone.

"Hello, this is His Holiness speaking. Get me Cardinal Gianelli in our Legal Department... Hello, Cardinal, you know the line in the Lord's Prayer, 'Give us this day our daily bread.' Well, how locked in are we on our contract with Pillsbury?"

A preacher wanted to raise money for his church and, being told that there was a fortune in horse racing, decided to purchase one and enter him in the races. However, at the local auction, the going prices for horses were so steep that the preacher ended up buying a donkey instead.

He figured that since he had it he might as well go ahead and enter it in the races, and, to his surprise, the donkey came in third. The next day, the racing forms carried this headline: PREACHER'S ASS SHOWS.

The preacher was so pleased with the donkey that he entered it in the races again. This time he won. The form read: PREACHER'S ASS OUT FRONT. The bishop was so upset with this kind of publicity he ordered the preacher not to enter the donkey in another race. The headline that day was: BISHOP SCRATCHES PREACHER'S ASS.

This was too much for the bishop and he ordered the preacher to get rid of the animal. The preacher decided to give the donkey to a nun in a nearby convent. The headline the next day read: NUN HAS BEST ASS IN TOWN. The bishop fainted. Then he informed the nun that she would have to dispose of the donkey. She finally found a farmer who was willing to buy the animal for ten dollars. The next day the headline stated: NUN PEDDLES ASS FOR TEN BUCKS.

They buried the bishop the next day.

GOVERNMENT BOND DESK,
DREXEL BURNHAM LAMBERT

The Ethics of Wall Street's Ethnic Humor

Hard as it may seem to believe, most of Wall Street's brokers and traders aren't the stereotypical square-jawed male WASP. In fact, if they were, Wall Street humor probably wouldn't exist, since the best jokes come from people making fun of themselves or their roots. WASP culture springs out of the Puritan work ethic (mind you, not *ethnic*), so it's rather dull and serious. That why most WASPs work in management at the middle and top floors of Wall Street's financial houses, leaving the make-it-or-break-it mind-set of the trading floors to those less repressed. So from the trading floor springs some of the best ethnic humor around, usually with the victim of the joke airing it first. Italians tell the best Italian jokes and Poles the best Polish jokes. As a result, everyone is eventually offended. But equally offended, since the humor cuts across just about every nation's border. Except Iceland's. Which explains the ethics of these ethnic jokes. While no one is around to be offended by an Icelandic joke, you can bet that no one is around to tell it either.

The following jokes are so popular, it is impossible for me to credit any specific source.

What do you get when you cross...
...a Mexican with an Oriental?
A car thief who can't drive

...a Mexican with an octopus?
I don't know, but it sure can pick lettuce.

...a Pole with a Chicano?
A kid who spray-paints his name on a chain link fence

...a Pole with a monkey?
Nothing. The monkey is too smart to screw a Pole.

...a black with a Sioux Indian?
A Sioux named boy

...a gay black with an Eskimo?
A snowblower that doesn't work

...a nigger with Bo Derek?
10 of spades

...a nigger and a chink?
A car thief who can't drive

...a nigger and a gorilla?
A dumb gorilla

. . . a Jew with a gypsy?
A chain of empty stores

. . . an Italian with a Mexican?
A guy who makes you an offer you can't understand

What are the four smallest books?

◇ *Italian War Heroes*
◇ *Who's Who in Poland*
◇ *Mexican Guide to Business Ethics*
◇ *Negro Yachtsmen I Have Known*

What do you call a Mexican baptism?
Bean dip

Did you hear about the Greek who left home because he didn't like the way he was being reared?

He went back because he couldn't leave his brother's behind.

What do you call two Vietnamese in a Trans Am?
The Gooks of Hazzard

Why are scientists breeding Mexicans instead of rats for experiments?

They multiply faster and you don't get attached to them.

Did you hear about the two Mexicans on "That's Incredible"?

One had auto insurance and the other was an only child.

What's six miles long and goes four miles an hour?

A Mexican funeral with only one set of jumper cables

Why did the cops take the 911 emergency number off the backs of their cars?

The Mexicans kept stealing them, thinking they were Porsches.

Why did they have to cancel drivers' education and sex education in Mexico?

The donkey died.

What do you call a Mexican with a vasectomy?

A dry Martinez

Why do Mexicans drive low riders?

So they can cruise and pick lettuce at the same time

How many Mexicans does it take to grease a car?

One, if you hit it right

What do Mexicans and cue balls have in common?

The more you hit 'em, the more English you get out of 'em.

Why don't Poles eat M&Ms?

They're too hard to peel.

How do you ruin a Polish party?

Flush the punch bowl.

Did you hear about the Polish abortion clinic?
It has a year-long waiting list.

How do you break a Pole's fingers?
Hit him in the nose.

What do you call a Pole with a lot of girl friends?
A shepherd

What happens when a Pole stops paying his garbage bill?
They stop delivering.

Did you hear about the Polish-American who couldn't spell?
He spent the night at the warehouse.

Why does the new Polish navy have glass-bottomed boats?
So they can see the old Polish navy

Why don't Poles make Kool-Aid?
They can't figure out how to get a quart of water into the envelope.

Why don't Poles get more than a half hour for lunch?
The bosses don't want to retrain them.

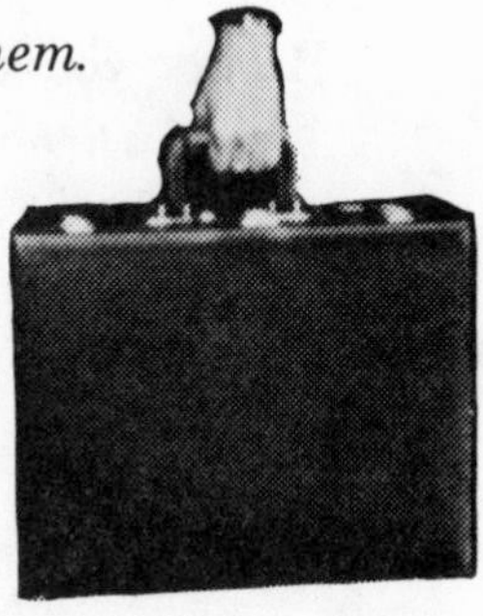

Did you hear about the Pole who studied five days for his urine test?

Did you hear about the Pole who thought asphalt was a rectal problem?

Did you hear about the Polish parachute?
It opens on impact.

What do you call a Pole with an IQ of 176?
A village

A Polish drug addict goes to a party with a bunch of other druggies. There's coke, crack, and pot, and the Pole's upset because he forgot his syringe. So he finds a needle someone else has discarded and is just about to shoot up when one of his friends says, "Don't do that. You might get AIDS."

"That's okay," says the Pole. "I'm wearing a condom."

Why do Poles wear rubbers on their ears?
So they don't get hearing aids

How do you keep a Pole busy for an hour?
Write "Turn over" on both sides of a dollar bill.

What do Poles do with their armies?
Put them in their sleevies.

A Pole says to his friend: "We have a tremendous bar in Brooklyn. Every tenth drink bought, a red light flashes on the cash register and whoever is paying for the drinks gets laid for nothing in the back room."

"Bet it never pays off," the friend says. "You ever won?"

"No, but my wife wins every time."

What do you call a skeleton in a closet?
A winner in a Polish game of hide-and-seek.

Have you heard about the Polish bank robber?
He tied up the safe and blew up the guard.

How do you get three Polacks off a couch?
Jerk one off and the other two come.

What do you call a pimple on a Polack's ass?
A brain tumor

How do you get a one-armed Polack out of a tree?
Wave to him.

Why don't they let Polacks swim across Lake Michigan?
Because they leave a ring

Why are there no gynecologists in Poland?
Because they can't read lips

Did you hear about the Polack who was found dead in his jail cell with twelve bumps on his head?
He tried to hang himself with a rubber band.

What's red, green, blue, yellow, purple, and orange?
A Polack all dressed up.

Did you hear there's a Polish Mafia?
They found two guys with their heads tied together and shot in their hands.

What did Christ tell the Poles when he was dying on the cross?
"Play dumb until I get back."

Did you hear about the stakes of the Polish lottery?
A dollar a year for a million years.

Why don't they use the 911 system in Poland?
Poles can't find the 11 on their telephone dials.

What's the difference between an Irish wedding and an Irish funeral?
One less drunk

Did you hear about the queer Irishman?
He preferred women over whiskey.

Why do blacks keep chickens?
To teach their kids how to walk

How do you make a black man nervous?
Take him to an auction.

What do you call a black man in a tree?
A branch manager

Why did the KKK buy the movie rights to *Roots*?
They can run it backwards so it has a happy ending.

Why do blacks keep their flies open?
In case they want to count to eleven

What do you call a black man in Thailand?
A tycoon

What's the difference between a nigger and a tire?
Tires don't sing when you put chains on them.

How do you keep five niggers from robbing a store?
Throw them a basketball.

Who are the suspects in the Atlanta killings?
An alligator disguised as a watermelon and the Son of Sambo

Why did God give niggers rhythm?
Because he fucked up their hair

What's the great white hope?
Sickle-cell anemia

What do you call a black test-tube baby?
Janitor in a drum

A nigger walks into a bar with a beautiful parrot on his shoulder. The bartender asks, "Where did you get that?"

The parrot says, "Africa."

What's black and shines in the dark?
Oakland

What do you call four niggers in a Cadillac?
Grand-theft auto

Did you ever see Ray Charles's wife?
Neither did he.

What do you call ten niggers on a white guy in Harlem?
A fair fight

What does it say inside a nigger's lips?
Inflate to 20 pounds.

Did you hear where Old Mother Hubbard, who lived in a shoe with so many children she didn't know what to do, moved?
To Atlanta

Why did the nigger marry a Mexican?
He didn't want his children to grow up too lazy to steal.

A black goes into an employment agency that guarantees that it is not prejudiced, but it administers an employment test. After four hours of the test, the black goes home and waits for his scores. A few days later, a memo comes back with the following note:

BIMM

GY

BAR

2PCT

The black shows his wife, and figures the news is good, that it means he's a black male, great looking, young, could make the bar, and in the upper two percent of the testing group. He calls the employment agency and tells them his analysis.

The professional says, "No, that's not it. It says, 'Be in Memphis Monday. Get Your Black Ass Ready to Pick Cotton Tuesday.' "

What's black, got six legs, and goes, "Ho-de-do, Ho-de-do"?
Three blacks running for an elevator

What's black, has white eyes, and knocks on glass?
A nigger in a microwave

What do you call lipstick for blacks?
Mop 'n' Glow

How did God make Puerto Ricans?
By sandblasting blacks

Who won the race down the tunnel, the black or the Pole?
The Pole, because the black had to stop and write "mother fucker" on the wall

What's the definition of worthless?
A seven-foot-two black man with a small cock who can't play basketball

How do you know Adam and Eve weren't black?
Ever try to take a rib away from a black man?

Did you hear about the little black kid who had diarrhea?
He thought he was melting.

Did you hear about the new black French restaurant?
Chez What?

What do you call four blacks in a '57 Chevy?
A blood vessel

Why do blacks wear white gloves?
So they don't bite off the ends of their fingers when they're eating Tootsie Rolls

Why does Georgia have blacks and California have earthquakes?

California had first pick.

Why don't black women make good nuns?

They can't say "superior" after "mother."

How many pall bearers do you need at a black man's funeral?

Five: four to carry the casket, and one to carry the radio.

What are three things you can't give a black man?

A black eye, a fat lip, or a job.

What do they do with dead blacks in Florida?

Debone them and sell them for wet suits.

What do you call a black nuclear physicist?

A nigger

How do you keep black kids from jumping on the bed?

Put Velcro on the ceiling.

How do you get them down?

Tell Spanish kids they are piñatas.

Did you hear about Firestein, the new brand of Jewish tires?

They not only stop on a dime, they pick it up.

How was the copper wire invented?
By two Jews fighting over a penny

What does a Jap do during a nuclear holocaust?
Get out a sun reflector.

How do you say "Fuck You" in Yiddish?
"Trust Me."

Why do Jews have such big noses?
Because air is free

What's a Jewish dilemma?
A free ham sandwich

If Tarzan and Jane were Jewish, what would Cheetah be?
A fur coat

How was the Grand Canyon formed?
A Jew dropped a nickel down a gopher hole.

Why do Italian men have mustaches?
So they'll look like their mothers

What's an innuendo?
An Italian suppository

Did you hear about the Italian who was asked to be a Jehovah's Witness?
He refused because he didn't see the accident.

How do you brainwash an Italian?
Give him an enema.

How do you get an Italian out of a bathtub?
Turn on the water.

Did you hear about the flamingos in Florida with little pink cement Italians on their lawns?

An Italian astronaut meets an American astronaut on the street. The American astronaut says he's leaving in two days for the moon, where he's going to collect rocks. The Italian says he's going to the sun.

"But you'll be burned up," says the American.

"Oh, that won't be a problem," answers the Italian. "I'm going at night."

Did you hear about the Italian who...

...spent four days in Sears looking for wheels for a miscarriage?

...took his expectant wife to the grocery store because they had free delivery?

...looked in a lumberyard for a draft board?

...took a roll of toilet paper to a crap game?

...put iodine on his paycheck because he got a cut in pay?

...was so lazy he married a pregnant woman?

...was feeling so low he got his face slapped?

...lost his girl friend because he couldn't remember where he laid her?

...wouldn't go out with his wife because she was a married woman?

...thought his typewriter was pregnant because it missed a period?

...wore a union suit because his wife was having labor pains?

...thought "no kidding" meant birth control?

...thought Peter Pan was something to put under the bed?

. . . who smelled good only on the right side, because he didn't know where to buy "Left Guard"?

. . . thought Moby Dick was a venereal disease?

. . . thought a mushroom was a place to neck?

. . . failed the Wasserman test?

How can you spot an Alitalia airplane?
From the hair under its wings

Why do Puerto Ricans throw away their garbage in clear plastic bags?
So Italians can go window-shopping

Did you hear Alitalia and El Al were merging to form a new airline?
It's going to be called "Well, I'll Tell Ya."

Why is Italy shaped like a boot?
Because they couldn't fit all that shit into a sneaker

Real Men Can't Eat Quiche

A real Wall Street hero is someone who is not only a millionaire a few times over, but an ex–fighter pilot. It's a macho, grace-under-pressure kind of thinking, and perpetuated by the fact that most Wall Streeters are ex-jocks who really do gag at quiche. Swish is just not In.

I heard these jokes from so many different people, it's not feasible to credit any one source.

What do gay men call hemorrhoids?
Speed bumps

What do you call a gay man in a wheelchair?
Rollaids

Did you hear the one about the queer deaf mute?
Neither did he.

What's the definition of confusion?
Twenty blind lesbians at a fish market

How do you separate the men from the boys in Greece?
With a crowbar

Did you hear about the queer who got fired from the sperm bank for drinking on the job?

Two gays live together. One works and the other doesn't. One morning, the one who works sees his lover ejaculating into a plastic bag in the kitchen. "What are you doing?" he asks him.

"Packing your lunch," his lover replies.

Did you hear about the queer burglar?

He couldn't blow the safe so he went down on the elevator.

How do you get four queers on a bar stool?

Turn it upside down.

What do you call two queers who go by the name of Bob?

Oral Roberts

What do gays call condoms?

Seal-A-Meal

Did you hear about the woman in San Francisco who was walking down the street and attacked by three men?

Two held her down while the other did her hair.

What's the difference between a priest and a homosexual?

The way they pronounce A-Men

Have you heard about the new disease gay musicians are coming down with?
Band-Aids

Did you hear about the two Irish gays?
Patrick Fitzhenry and Henry Fitzpatrick

Did you hear about the new breakfast cereal called Queerios?
Add milk and they eat themselves.

What do you call a gay dentist?
Tooth fairy

What's a gay Jew?
A Heblew

And the Beat Goes On . . .

The world of publishing, alas, lags the real world, so in an effort to keep current, I continued collecting jokes even as this book was in the process of making its way through rounds of editors. Even so, it's impossible to keep up with Wall Street's humor, since its velocity equals the speed of sound and its volume is right up there with the number of shares traded.

STOCKS PLUNGE 508 POINTS, A DROP OF 22.6%,
WORLDWIDE IMPACT
***New York Times,* October 20, 1987**

After Black Monday, traders faced two options. What were they?

One bullet or two?

A client who faced tremendous losses called his broker, who wasn't there. When asked what had happened to the broker, the receptionist said, "He died in a plane crash." The next day, the client calls back. "He died in a plane crash," said the same receptionist. The next day, the client calls again and asks where the broker is. "Don't you believe me?" asks the receptionist. "I've told you three times he's died in a plane crash."

"Oh, I believe you," said the client. "I just love hearing it."

What do you call a Salomon Brothers trader?
A waiter

What do you call his lawyer?
A busboy

What's the difference between the crash of 1987 and the crash of 1929?
Now the computers are jumping out of the windows.

What did the hotel clerk ask the broker when he wanted a room at the Hyatt?
"Is it for sleeping or jumping?"

Why haven't more brokers taken the plunge?
They can't open the windows.

What is the probability of precipitation?
Rain, 30 percent; brokers, 70.

How do you get a broker down from a tree?

Cut the rope

What's the best way to make a million dollars in the stock market?

Start with two million

What's the difference between a stockbroker and a pigeon?

A pigeon can still make a deposit on a BMW.

How many stockbrokers can you put in the back of a pickup?

Only two. You have to leave room for their lawnmowers.

What's the difference between a skunk and a broker on the road?

There are skid marks before the skunk.

Did you hear about the new Yuppie disease, RAIDS?

Recently Acquired Income Deficiency Syndrome.

You get it through casual contact with common stock.

Biden Admits Plagiarism in School, but Not in Political Speechmaking
***New York Times,* September 18, 1987**

What did Biden have to say about the market panic?

"We have nothing to fear but fear itself."

Did you see Biden sitting behind the pope when he spoke at the stadium?

He was taking notes for his next speech.

What's the name of Biden's new autobiography?

Iaccoca

Jimmy Carter, Richard Nixon, Gary Hart, Joe Biden, and Michael Dukakis are all on a boat that explodes. They get out the lifeboats and Carter screams: "Women first."

Nixon yells: "Fuck the women."

Hart asks: "Is there time?"

Biden asks: "Is there time?"

And Dukakis says: "Did you hear what Biden said?"

Nancy Reagan Faces Breast Cancer Surgery

***New York Times,* October 16, 1987**

What has two tits and eight legs?
The Fords and Reagans on a double date

Do you know why Ronald Reagan didn't notice the market collapse?
Because Nancy had gone flat the week before.

Did you hear Nancy Reagan sued her surgeon?

- ◊ *He took the wrong boob out of the White House*
- ◊ *There are still two boobs left in the White House.*

What does Gary Hart's re-entry in the presidential race prove?
It just goes to show that you really can fuck your brains out.

What does Hart have to do if he becomes president?
Put his private assets in a blind trust.

What did Gary Hart say to Donna Rice?
"I said sit on my face, not ruin my race."

What is the difference between a Republican woman and a Democratic woman?

A Republican has her heart in Bush while a Democrat has her bush in Hart.

Aside from news events, the usual double-edged humor continues to make the rounds....

What do you get when you cross a pit bull and a prostitute?

Your last blow job ever

What do you call Oprah Winfrey with a yeast infection?

A whopper with cheese

What did Oprah Winfrey's boyfriend say to her when he wanted her to change sexual positions?

"How now, brown cow."

Did you hear they got Oprah Winfrey for drug smuggling?

They lifted her dress and found ninety pounds of crack.

A man complains to his doctor that he doesn't know if his wife has Alzheimer's disease or AIDS. "I don't know what to do," he says.

"Well," the doctor advises, "when your wife comes home, tell her to walk around the block twice, and if she comes home, don't fuck her."

How do you fuck an ugly girl?
Jerk off on your hand and throw it at her.

How do we know that Christa McAuliffe had dandruff?
Her head and shoulders washed up on the beach.

How do you get gerbils out of a tree?
Moon them.

What do you call a girl with one leg?
Peg

What do you call a girl with a glass eye?
Crystal

What do you call a man hanging off a ledge?
Cliff

A couple goes to a hotel in the Poconos and rents the honeymoon suite. But just after they arrive, the desk clerk notices that the groom goes out fishing.

The next day, the groom once again goes fishing until nightfall. The same thing happens the next day and the next. The following morning, the clerk asks the husband why he is leaving his new wife so much.

"Well, she has gonorrhea," he says.

"Well, why not have oral sex?" asks the clerk.

The groom shakes his head. "No, she has pyorrhea."

"That's too bad," says the clerk.

The groom shrugs and says, "Not really. She also has worms and I like to go fishing."

What does the Army and a blow job have in common?

The closer you get to discharge, the better it feels.

Three mothers are talking about their sons. The first one brags "My son went to Harvard Medical School and he's now head of surgery at Mount Sinai."

The second one says, "My son went to Yale, then Harvard Business School, and now he's a managing director at Salomon Brothers."

The third hangs her head and says "My son isn't doing so good. He got into drugs in college, he dropped out of school, and he just told me he's gay and living with not one but two lovers in New York. One's the head of surgery at Mount Sinai and the other is a managing director at Salomon Brothers.

A husband and wife are hiking and the husband goes to pee in the bushes. Just as he's done, a snake comes out and bites his penis.

"Hurry, get a doctor," he yells to his wife.

She runs to the center of town and the doctor tells her if she doesn't suck the poision out, her husband won't have long to live. She runs back to her husband.

"What did the doctor say?" he asks.

"You're going to die," she replies.

A man goes in search of his golf ball in the woods at his local country club and stumbles across a leprechaun. "Since you found me, you have one wish," says the leprechaun to the golfer.

"I want to be a really great golfer," says the man.

The leprechaun says, "Puff, you're a really great golfer now, but this is one wish there's a problem with. It may negatively affect your sex life."

The man shrugs and returns to his game. In the following year, he plays perfect golf, and another year later, he's back on the same hole at his country club and stumbles across the leprechaun again.

"Hey, thanks for granting that wish," he tells the leprechaun. "I'm as good as the pros."

"But what about your sex life?" asks the leprechaun. "What about the side effects?"

"Well," the man replies, "I had a woman once before Christmas, then another in May, but that's not too bad for a priest.

Faced with huge stock market losses, a wealthy man goes back to his penthouse and tells his wife, "Listen, honey, we have to cut down on spending. We'll have to get rid of the cook, the chauffeur, and the house in East Hampton." She's so shook up that she jumps out of the window. What does her husband scream?

"Thank you, PaineWebber."

And as investment firms started to merge, as well as lay-off employees, here's a sample of some of the jokes that went around....

What would you call a merger between PaineWebber and Shearson Lehman Brothers?

Shear Paine

What's the new definition of a Yuppie?

Young Unemployed Previously Prosperous Inexperienced Executive

What's the difference between Salomon Brothers and other Wall Street firms?

About two months

Did you hear that Jimmy Swaggart and Jim Bakker are going to star in a movie together?

It's called Children of a Looser God.